Wolves

Einstein Sisters

KidsWorld

About Wolves

Grey Wolf

There is something magical about a wolf's howl.
It makes you think about living free in
the wild. The wolf is respected and honored
by almost every native culture
in North America.

Red Wolf

The two main species of wolf in **North America** are the **grey wolf** and the **red wolf**.

Red Wolf

The red wolf is smaller than the grey wolf but bigger than the coyote.

It has mostly brownish fur with some grey or black mixed in and red fur on its face, ears and legs.

Red wolves
live in many habitats,
from forests to
swampy areas.

There used to be **more than 100,000** red wolves living in the wild. Today only about **70 are left in the wild** and about **200 live in captivity.**

Some people think the red wolf is not a true wolf. They think it is a mixture of grey wolf and coyote.

Red wolves eat white-tailed deer and smaller animals like raccoons, nutria, rabbits and mice.

Nutria

The grey wolf is the most **common** type of wolf in the **world**.

There are many different **subspecies (types)** of **grey wolf**.

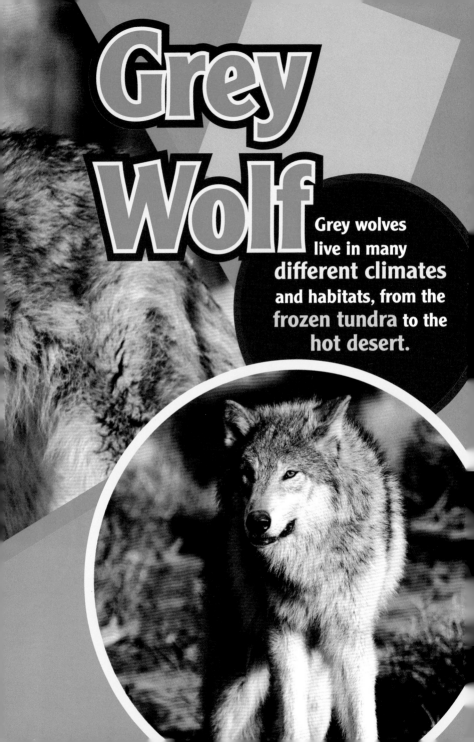

Grey Wolf

Grey wolves live in many **different climates** and habitats, from the frozen tundra to the hot desert.

Arctic Wolf

The type of **grey wolf** that lives in the tundra is the **arctic wolf.**

They have **shorter** legs, **smaller** ears and **thicker** fur, which helps them **stay warm** in their **freezing habitat**.

Arctic wolves are smaller than ordinary **grey wolves**.

It's thick, **white** coat lets the wolf **blend in** with the snowy ground.

The **arctic wolf** ranges from Alaska, through northern **Canada** and into **Greenland.**

Arctic wolves eat mostly **musk oxen**, caribou and **arctic hares**, but sometimes also **lemmings** **and birds.**

The **Mexican wolf** is a subspecies of grey wolf that lives in the desert of **Mexico, New Mexico** and **Arizona**.

Mexican Wolf

It is the **most endangered subspecies** of grey wolf in the world. Not long ago no Mexican wolves were left in the wild in the U.S. **Today there are about 80.**

The **Mexican wolf** is also known as **El lobo.**

Different types of grey wolves live in **Europe** and **Asia**.

The **Eurasian wolf** is the most common subspecies. It used to live all over **Europe** and **Asia** but was killed off in many places where it lived.

The **Iberian wolf** lives only in Portugal and Spain. It is **smaller** than the Eurasian wolf.

The **Iberian wolf** has a white patch on each side of its **muzzle** and **black** lines on its front legs.

And some scientists think the **Ethiopian wolf** might be a type of jackal.

The Ethiopian wolf is the most **endangered** carnivore in Africa.

Australia's wild dog, the **dingo**, is a subspecies of the **grey wolf.**

All pet **dogs** today are a subspecies of the **grey wolf.**

Some still **look** a lot like **wolves.**

Some **not so much.**

A grey wolf's fur can be grey, brown, white, **reddish** or **black**.

Black wolves are becoming more **common** in North America, but they are **rare** in Europe or Asia. The **black** colored fur may have come from **domestic dogs** that mated with **wolves**.

Wolves in the same **pack** do not always have the same color fur. Even **pups** from the **same litter** are **not always the same color.**

Coyotes look a lot like grey wolves. It can be hard to tell them apart, but there are a few clues you can look for.

Wolves are **bigger**. They can weigh **twice as much** as a **coyote** does.

A **coyote's** ears are **bigger** and are **pointed**. A **wolf's** ears look **smaller** and are **rounded**.

A **coyote** has a pointier, slimmer **snout** and a smaller **nose**.

Wolves walk and run on their toes. They can move faster than animals that walk flat on their feet. It also lets them turn quickly.

The **fur** between a wolf's toes keeps its feet from **freezing** when it walks **on snow** and ice.

A wolf's **toes** spread away from each other when the **wolf** steps down.

This gives the wolf a good **grip**.

Wolves have 42 teeth. Their sharp canine teeth are used for grabbing and killing prey. Their back teeth can crush bone.

The rest of their teeth are used to tear meat away from bones.

Wolves do not chew their food. They bite off chunks and swallow them whole.

That's where the expression "wolfing down your food" came from.

Wolves live in groups called **packs.**

The **alpha** male and female stay **together for life.** Other members of the pack may **leave the pack.**

Wolf Packs

A pack is a family unit. It is made up of the alpha male, the alpha female and their young. Members of the same pack are called pack mates.

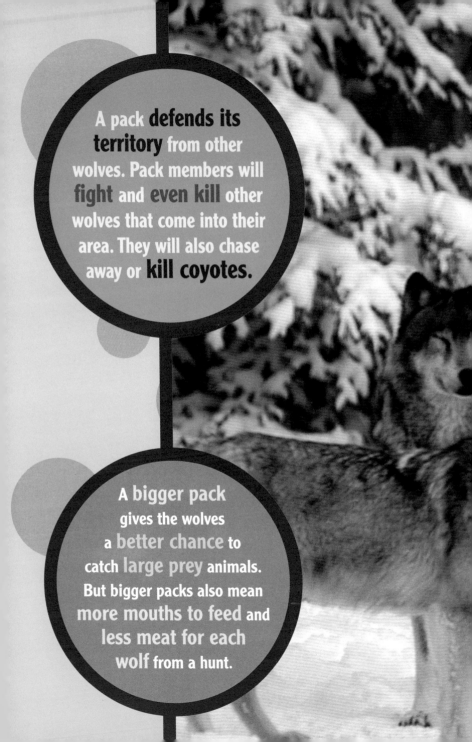

A pack **defends its territory** from other wolves. Pack members will **fight** and **even kill** other wolves that come into their area. They will also chase away or **kill coyotes.**

A **bigger pack** gives the wolves a better chance to catch large prey animals. But bigger packs also mean more mouths to feed and less meat for each wolf from a hunt.

The size of a pack depends on **how much food is available.** Most packs have from **4 to 10 wolves.** In places with lots of prey, packs can have up to **20 members.**

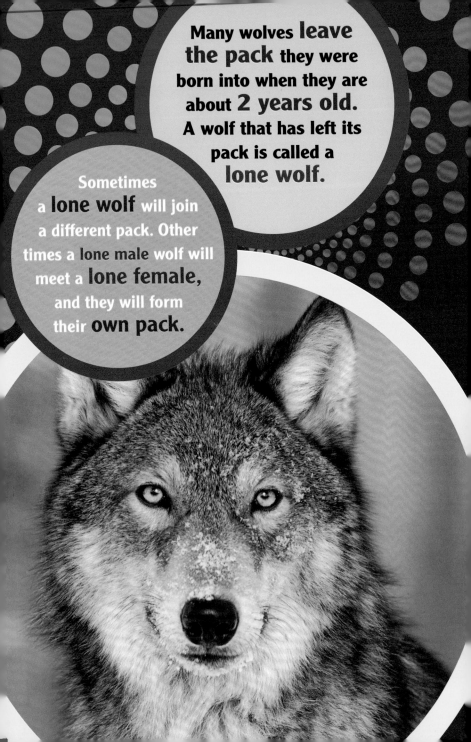

Many wolves **leave the pack** they were born into when they are about **2 years old.** A wolf that has left its pack is called a **lone wolf.**

Sometimes a **lone wolf** will join a different pack. Other times a lone male wolf will meet a **lone female,** and they will form their **own pack.**

Sometimes a lone wolf does not become a member of a pack at all.

A wolf with no pack does not have its own territory. It must live sneakily in other packs' territories being careful not to get caught in their space.

Wolves are **famous** for their **howl.** The sound of a wolf's howl can be heard **more than** 100 city blocks away.

They **howl** to keep in touch with the rest of their pack. They also howl to **warn other wolves** away from their territory. Packs will also howl together **before a hunt.**

Wolves usually do not **howl** when it is **raining hard** or **very windy. The sound** of their voices **do not travel as far** in the wind or rain.

Wolves do not actually **howl at the moon.** That is a **myth.** It just looks like they do because they **raise their head to howl.**

Wolves also "talk" to each other with body language.

A wolf with flat ears, a wrinkled snout and its lips pulled back from its teeth is sending a clear warning.

Wolves that want to play will do a "play bow" to get a game started.

Wolves in a pack spend a lot of time playing together. Pups like to play fight, wrestle and play with sticks, bones and feathers.

Playing together keeps a pack's **bonds** strong. It also helps the wolves practice the **skills** they need for hunting.

Even **adult** pack mates like to play games of **chase** and **wrestle**.

Wolves are long-distance runners. They can run for **hours** at a quick, steady speed without getting tired.

They can usually **smell** their **prey** before they see it. They **follow the scent** to find the prey and then chase it until it is **too tired** to get away.

A wolf's **sense of smell** is about **100 times** better than a **human's.**

A wolf pack hunts as a group to catch large prey like **deer, moose, elk** and **bison.** The alpha male and female are the **best hunters.**

Wolves are **mostly nocturnal,** meaning they are more active at night. They usually start **hunting at dusk.**

Wolves sometimes have to go **many days without eating.** Only about **1 in 10 hunts** ends in a kill.

Some wolves in British Columbia go to the sea to find their prey. They eat fish, sea birds and even seals that are sunning themselves on the shore or on rocks.

The amount of **meat** an adult wolf can eat in **one meal** would be as much as **80 hamburgers!**

When a **pack** can't catch a large prey animal to share, **every member hunts** on its own. Wolves hunting alone eat small animals like **rabbits, hares** and **beavers.**

Lone wolves that are not part of a pack also **hunt small prey.**

After a **big meal, wolves** don't need to **eat** again for **a few days.**

When **hunting in snow**, wolves often move in **single file**. The wolf behind steps in the footprints of the wolf ahead **to save energy**.

The **alpha wolf** goes **first** and sets the path for the **rest** to follow.

The **smallest wolves** are at the end of the line. The **trail is then packed down** and **easier** for them to **walk on**.

A **wolf pup** is born with blue eyes. Its eyes change colour as the wolf gets **older**. Adult wolves usually have amber eyes.

Its **eyes** open when it is about **11 to 14 days old**, but it takes a few more weeks before the pup can see properly.

A **pup's ears** are small and floppy when it is born. After about **3 weeks**, the ears start to straighten so the pup can hear better.

Wolf pups are **deaf** and **blind** when they are **born**.

Wolves use **dens** only when the pups are **too young to move** with the rest of the **pack.**

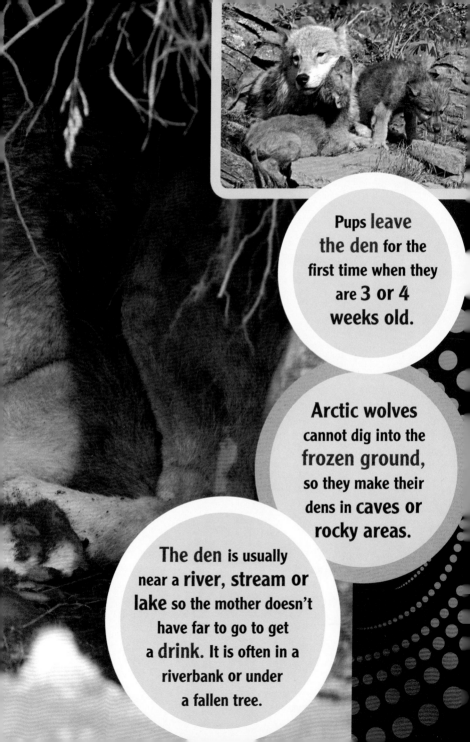

Pups leave the den for the first time when they are 3 or 4 weeks old.

Arctic wolves cannot dig into the frozen ground, so they make their dens in caves or rocky areas.

The den is usually near a river, stream or lake so the mother doesn't have far to go to get a drink. It is often in a riverbank or under a fallen tree.

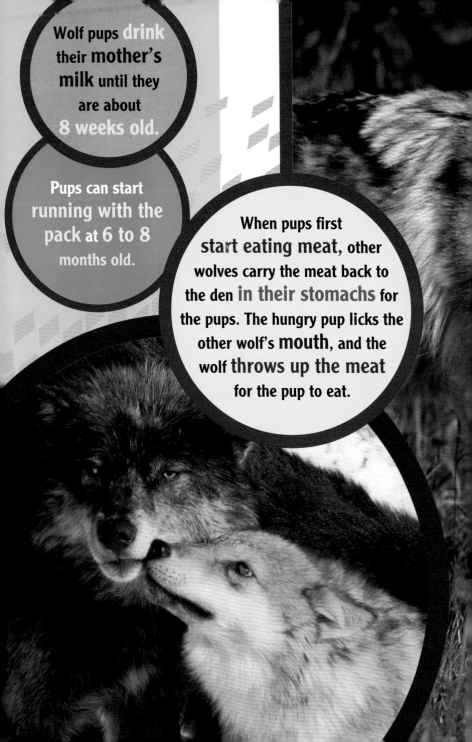

Wolf pups **drink** their **mother's milk** until they are about **8 weeks old.**

Pups can start **running with the pack at 6 to 8** months old.

When pups first **start eating meat,** other wolves carry the meat back to the den **in their stomachs** for the pups. The hungry pup licks the other wolf's **mouth,** and the wolf **throws up the meat** for the pup to eat.

Older pups that can't hunt with the pack stay at "rendezvous sites" with a babysitter. After the hunt, the pack meets up at this site. It is often a big field.

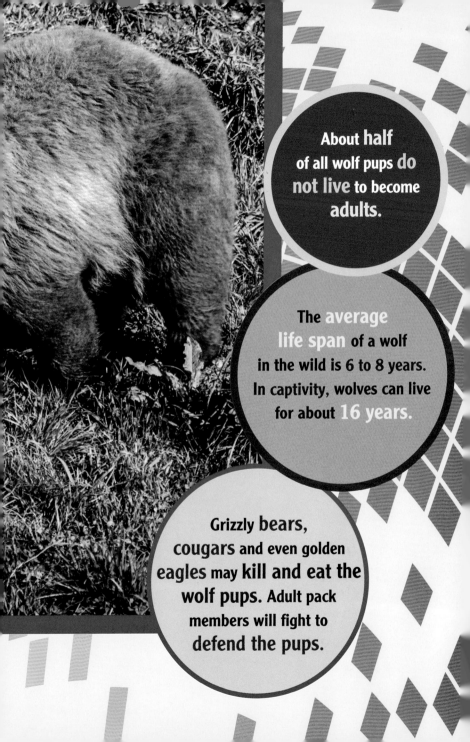

About **half** of all wolf pups do **not live** to become **adults.**

The **average life span** of a wolf in the wild is 6 to 8 years. In captivity, wolves can live for about **16 years.**

Grizzly **bears,** **cougars** and even golden eagles may **kill and eat the wolf pups.** Adult pack members will fight to **defend the pups.**

In the past many people **feared wolves**. They were afraid of being **attacked**, so they **killed** any wolves they saw.

Ranchers and farmers killed many wolves because they were **afraid** the wolves would **prey** on their **cows**, **sheep** and **chickens**.

Many hunters don't like wolves because **wolves kill the same species** the hunters want. They are afraid there will not be enough **animals** left for them if **wolves are hunting** them too.

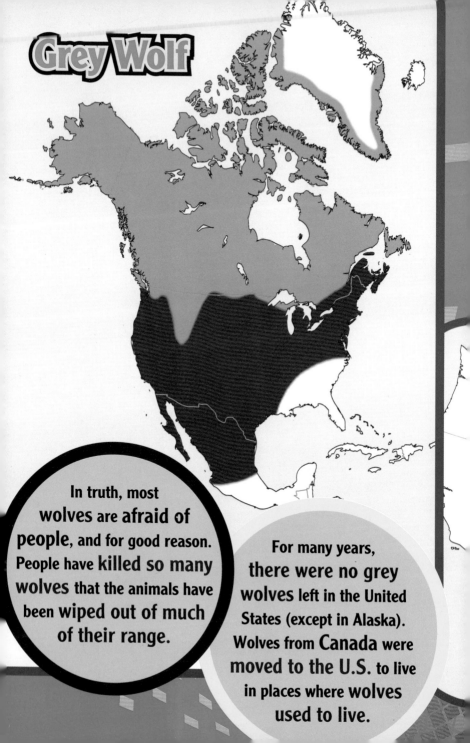

Grey Wolf

In truth, most **wolves** are **afraid of people**, and for good reason. People have **killed so many** wolves that the animals have been **wiped out of much of their range.**

For many years, **there were no grey wolves left in the United States** (except in Alaska). **Wolves from Canada** were **moved to the U.S. to live** in places where **wolves used to live.**

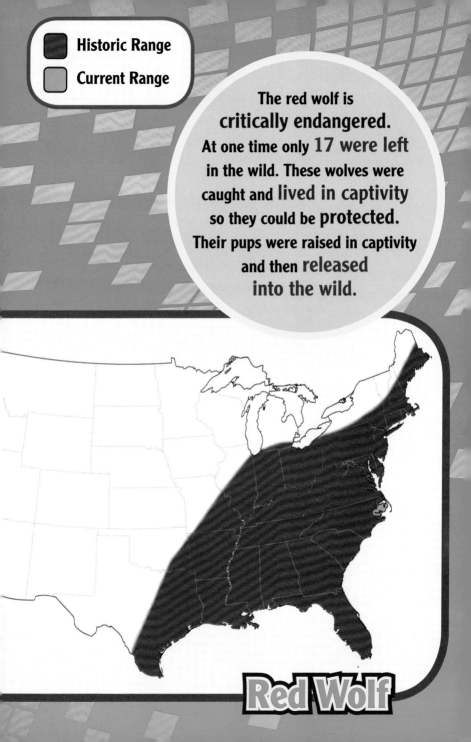

Historic Range

Current Range

The red wolf is **critically endangered.** At one time only **17 were left** in the wild. These wolves were caught and **lived in captivity** so they could be **protected.** Their pups were raised in captivity and then **released** into the wild.

Red Wolf

Scientists now realize that wolves are an important part of an ecosystem. In fact, wolves are what is known as a "keystone species." This means that the ecosystem is healthier with wolves in it.

Many other animals, like ravens, coyotes, foxes and even bears, feed on wolf kills.

Wolves help control the number of grazers, like deer and elk, in an area. If there are too many grazers, they eat all the plants.

The Publisher: KidsWorld Books

Library and Archives Canada Cataloguing in Publication

Wolves (Vancouver B.C.)
  Wolves / Einstein Sisters.

ISBN 978-1-988183-10-7 (softcover)

  1. Wolves—Juvenile literature. I. Einstein Sisters, author II. Title.

QL737.C22W647 2017   j599.773   C2016-907487-0

Cover Images: Front cover: From Thinkstock, Tom Brakefield
Back cover: From Thinkstock: mirceax, Hemera Technologies, jeanro

Background graphics: abstract swirl shape, hakkiarslan/ Thinkstock, 13, 16, 20, 22, 24, 27, 32, 34, 40, 48–49, 50, 52; abstract background, Maryna Borysevych, 11, 31, 36, 43, 44; pixels, Misko Kordic, 3, 5, 14, 18, 28, 38, 47, 56, 59, 60.

Maps: base map, erind, 60, 61; map, Tamara Hartson, 60, 61.

Photo credits: From Thinkstock: afhunta, 21; AlanJeffery 16–17; Andy_Astbury 46–47; Anolis01, 7; Debraansky, 63; DeMaster, 6; Design Pics, 53; Donyanedomam, 9; edouard rozey 3; Glenn Nagel, 37; Hemera Technologies, 13, 36; Holly Kuchera, 24, 34; jean-edouard rozey, 4; Jeff McGraw, 62–63; John Alves, 26, 40, 41; John Pitcher, 22–23, 35, 50–51; John_Wijsman, 22; JohnDPorter, p. 38; Jonathan Lyons, 5; Jupiterimages, 21, 32–33, 39, 44–45; kangarooarts, 43, 56–57; karlumbriaco, 8, 10–11, 12, 52–53; Len Jellicoe, 25; LuCaAr, 19; Lynn_Bystrom, p. 51; MikeLane45, 42; mirceax 2, 10; Pavel Losevsky, 28–29; PeakMystique, 14; photos_martYmage, 13; Pi-Lens, 27; PobladuraFCG, 17; Purestock, p. 58; RamiroMarquezPhotos, 30–31; Tom Brakefield, 18, 54–55; twildlif, 15e; weisen007, 48–49; Whitepointer, 20; Zeke1, 50, 52, 54, 59.

We acknowledge the financial support of the Government of Canada.

Funded by the Government of Canada
Financé par le gouvernement du Canada | Canadä

PC: 28